Y0-BQW-684

Boise State University Western Writers Series   Number 91

John Graves

By Dorys Crow Grover

East Texas State University

74565

Editors: Wayne Chatterton
James H. Maguire

Business Manager:
James Hadden

Cover Design and Illustration
by Arny Skov, Copyright 1989

Boise State University, Boise, Idaho

Library of Congress Card No. 89-60064

International Standard Book No. 0-88430-090-0

Printed in the United States of America by
Boise State University Printing and Graphics Services
Boise, Idaho

John Graves

John Graves

John Graves, a Texas-born naturalist, visited the Brazos River in north-central Texas in 1957, after a decade of world wandering, and wrote a farewell to a river, a book that has become a pastoral classic in American *belles-lettres*. *Goodbye to a River* has since been joined by two other nature volumes, and all three have earned for Graves a considerable reputation for his literary style. M. E. Bradford writes that Graves's voice is "deceptively simple and disarmingly personal in its flavor" ("John Graves" 142). In his craft, he joins fellow Texans Roy Bedichek and J. Frank Dobie, and his name should be added to the list of contemporary nature writers—including Edward Abbey, Annie Dillard, Louis Bromfield, John McPhee, and Gary Snyder—for he has inherited that peculiar combination of autobiography, natural history, and philosophy which can be traced to early naturalists William Bartram, Henry David Thoreau, and John Muir.

In an ecological sense, and as a landsman working his home-owned ground, he belongs with the front-rank nature writers in his ruminations and observations about life in the edgelands or rural country rather than in a frontier wilderness. His three books—*Goodbye to a River: A Narrative* (1960), *Hard Scrabble: Observations on a Patch of Land* (1974), *From a Limestone Ledge: Some Essays and Other Ruminations about Country Life in Texas* (1980)—form his Brazos trilogy founded on research into the natural history and myth of his region of north-central Texas.

Not all of Graves's writings are set in Texas. His short stories, essays, and articles move from the Southwest to New York City, Mexico, Spain, and the South Pacific. A craftsman of the English language, he is also fluent in Spanish and adept in recording Southwestern American rural dialects. Throughout his Brazos trilogy, Graves is conscious of his own fallibility in an unfriendly if not often hostile environment, and he admits he encounters problems he cannot always solve.

Some critics have called him the Thoreau of Texas—a comparison also given to Bedichek, one of a triumvirate which included Dobie and Walter Prescott Webb, the trio who for years dominated Texas letters. All these writers have similar attitudes toward humankind's aggressive land ownership; and although Graves becomes "owner" of a part of the earth's surface, he believes a person can own the land only in his head. Thoreau likewise prefers that a place not own one. Another similarity critics find between Graves and Thoreau is in their river books. Both authors make similar speculations about the history and legends of their rivers: Graves in *Goodbye to a River*, and Thoreau in *A Week on the Concord and Merrimack Rivers*. If Graves is a literary kin of Thoreau, the kinship may consist not only of common understanding of some of nature's secrets (which both have relayed to their readers) but also of their conversion of a river excursion into a memorable saga.

Like Thoreau and Bedichek, Graves brings to his prose a subtle wit, understated and provocative. Bedichek's prose is often marked by increasing anger and concern about the mistreatment of nature by land developers, oilmen, and builders of dams. Just so, he is curious and meditative about wildlife and nature. Graves has similar complaints against those destroying the natural wild but seems to have little hope for better management of the natural resources. Like Bedichek, he too meditates and speculates about nature.

From Dobie, who took the Southwestern storytellers as his models and who was an observer of animal life, Graves learned that personal experience can be rightfully told and enlarged upon through folklore. And from Webb and other historians, Graves learned that historical fact can be combined with folklore and natural history writing.

Bedichek, Dobie, and Webb—the three "Holy Oldtimers," as Larry McMurtry calls them—were influential on a number of Texas writers; and in a 1983 symposium address titled "The Texas Literary Tradition: Fiction, Folklore, History," Graves referred to his three Texas precursors as "The Old Guard" and noted they were "sensitive creators" who influenced him and laid the foundation for a rural, natural quality of Texas literature. "They believed in the dependence on nature," Graves said, adding that he and the "old guard" belong to the same fraternity. If Graves worries about finding the right thing to put into his books, he is little different from Bedichek who, when writing *Adventures with a Texas Naturalist* (1947), told Dobie he was worried about finding enough material to have some sort of unity. In response to Dobie's call for the necessity of the universal in local particularity, Graves has met the challenge.

Many factors have led John Graves to the position he holds as the current Dean of Texas writers. He was born in Fort Worth on 6 August 1920, and he grew up there. With boyhood friends, he explored the Trinity River bottoms when they were wild and less settled than they are today and when they provided good hunting. Frequently he and his friends went as far as the Brazos River where, under the guidance of a Negro woodsman, they learned to camp, hunt, and fish. During these years Graves cultivated an affection for the woods and rivers that has remained with him.

After finishing high school in Fort Worth, he attended Rice University in Houston where he studied under George Williams, a noteworthy teacher and writer. When Graves was interviewed by Patrick Bennett for *Talking with Texas Writers* (1980) and Bennett asked him about his writing style, he spoke of being encouraged by Williams and noted that Williams had been an influence on other Texans, including McMurtry, J. P. Miller, and William Goyen, all of whom were at Rice at one time or another. After graduating from Rice with Phi Beta Kappa honors and a Bachelor of Arts degree in 1942, Graves went to Marine Corps officers' school and was shipped to the Pacific as a first lieutenant in the Fourth Marine Division. Wounded on Saipan, he received the Purple Heart and was sent home. He attained the rank of Captain; and when offered the chance of staying in the regular Marine Corps, he decided against it, but he is presently an officer in the reserve.

Graves lived for a while in Mexico, but in 1946 he went to New York City and started work on a master's degree at Columbia University. He enrolled in a writing class taught by Martha Foley, a short story writer and longtime editor of *Story Magazine*, as well as editor of *The Best American Short Stories*. Graves has said that this was when he became serious about writing. While in Foley's class, he sold one of his first stories, "Quarry," to the *New Yorker* in 1947.

Graves was awarded the master's degree from Columbia in 1948 and that same year he began teaching English at the University of Texas, Austin. Dissatisfied with the routine of teaching, he left Austin in 1950 and began a decade of drifting. His first marriage ended in 1952. His desire to write, as well as his interest in traveling, led him to New Mexico, New York, France, Spain, and other places. He established a writing connection with *Holiday* magazine and lived abroad, mostly in Spain, and he says that Spain cleansed him in terms of his work.

Before going to Madrid, he spent some time in Majorca, but

in Madrid he ran into Jim Phillips, a Texas novelist, who told him about the Canary Islands and the resident colony of writers, artists, and newspaper people at Tenerife. Graves spent some pleasant months in Tenerife before he returned to the United States, where he was located for a time at Sag Harbor. Then for a few months he lived in Mexico.

In 1958 he joined the faculty of Texas Christian University as a teacher of creative writing, but he left TCU in 1965 to continue writing. When awarded an honorary Doctor of Letters degree in 1983 by the Board of Trustees and the Chancellor of Texas Christian University, Graves was cited (according to TCU English professor Robert Frye) as follows:

Farmer and Phi Beta Kappa, decorated Marine and cogent conservationist, river historian and raconteur extraordinary. . . . and above all a gifted writer who sees life steadily and sees it whole. Viewing nature with mystical fascination leavened with bracing candor, he reminds us of our roots, enlarges our sense of place, and urges us toward being entire, whole.

Graves has an abiding connection with Texas Christian University, not only because he was on the faculty there for seven years and received the honorary degree, but also because he was the honored speaker for the annual Cecil B. Williams Memorial lecture and Creative Writing Day convocation in 1979.

The university *Citation* is in reference to lines from *Hard Scrabble*, for there Graves perceives "all things natural and rural being parts of a whole," and we become keenly conscious that in nature there is "a whole and single Way whose intricacies no man truly knows" (113). Like Gerard Manley Hopkins, Graves would have us find joy in the diversity of copious creation and appreciate the essential unity of the world around us.

It was the autumn of 1957 when Graves made the canoe trip down a portion of the Brazos River and began writing what became *Goodbye to a River*. With the proceeds from the sale of his river book, he purchased the first of his limestone acres near Glen Rose in 1960. Intending to use the place as a weekend retreat, he sank a well, put in a pump and a storage tank, and built a stone house. He tells in *Hard Scrabble* about the labor he expended to bring his place into production.

Meanwhile, when Stuart Udall, Secretary of the Interior under Presidents John F. Kennedy and Lyndon B. Johnson, appointed a team to investigate the pollution of the Potomac River, Graves was invited to participate in the study. As a result of that experience, he contributed "A River and a Piece of Country: A Potomac Essay," to the *Potomac Interim Report to the President*, which also included essays by other members of the task force. Somewhat dissatisfied with the *Interim Report*, he published *The Creek and the City*, a report on Rock Creek and Metropolitan Washington. The final official task force report was *The Nation's River* (1968), to which Graves and several others contributed.

Upon his return to Texas, Graves added to his stone house, and in 1970 he moved there with his second wife, the attractive, dark-haired Jane Marshall Cole, formerly of New York City, and their two daughters, Helen and Sally. Here he does his writing, and when he writes he works in a corner of the big, open barn, in a room lined with shelves full of books. In most barns this would be a tack room where saddles and riding gear are kept, but Graves keeps some of his books here and they are of a variety, with many technical books dealing with water problems, cattle breeding, bee keeping, irrigation, and growing crops.

Graves makes clear in *Hard Scrabble* his admiration for those who are good stewards of the soil. He is himself a stock rancher, and his essays in *From a Limestone Ledge* reveal his love of the rustic life. In an interview with Claire Eyrich of the *Fort Worth Star-Telegram*, he says, "I wanted to be a farmer; to do it all" (1). Limestone acres are not the easiest to maintain, but Graves, like Sophocles, is ultimately and essentially affirmative in his outlook on life, retaining hope despite the hardships. As he remarks in *Hard Scrabble*, "good people do turn up" (144). Graves's conservation practices are evident in his ranching operation, and he carefully plans the development and use of his land to its best potential. While he may be, as he describes himself in *Hard Scrabble*, an "inveterate romantic," he is not a sentimental refugee from the city who is unaware of the harsh realities of rural life.

In his thoughtful and provocative essays, Graves looks at the realities of life which others often interpret as technological progress, and although he is keenly aware of the trials and stresses of living in a rapidly changing machine-centered world, he prefers to concentrate on a nature-centered world which can bring to mankind some sense of order and peace. Not a polemicist, he would have us remain true to ourselves and retain our attachment to the land.

In addition to his three books, Graves has written several short stories and many essays for various magazines, including *American Heritage, Atlantic, Esquire, Holiday, New Yorker*, and *Town and Country*. He has served as contributing editor for *Southwest Review* and is presently a contributing editor for *Texas Monthly*, a popular magazine devoted to the critical and impartial discussion of economic, political, and social questions of Texas and its place in the nation and the world. The magazine is separate from Texas Monthly Press, which has reprinted several of his books.

Graves was the recipient of a Guggenheim fellowship in 1963 and a Rockefeller in 1972. In 1983 he received the prestigious McCombs-Tinkle award for continuing excellence in Texas letters,

11

an award that has been given to only a few others. He is a fellow and former president of the Texas Institute of Letters. In 1984 he was recognized as a distinguished alumnus of Rice University. From his home on the Brazos, Graves continues to receive awards for the achievements of a career that began more than forty years ago.

Graves began his writing career with short fiction, and some of his stories are set in Texas, but several have sites in foreign lands. Although he is a good fiction writer, he is better as a nature writer because his nonfiction prose style is fresher and he seems more relaxed when writing the essay. Although he has moved away from fiction, he told Bennett in 1980 he has in a trunk one finished novel and one unfinished, the latter begun under the 1983 Guggenheim fellowship (67).

His first story, "Quarry," is set in New York and is about a mouse captured alive by two apartment dwellers who keep it overnight in a box while they decide what to do with it. They do not want to let it go, but neither can they kill it. The next morning they decide to free it, but by then it is too late. Hunched and addled in the box, the mouse no longer looks like itself, and when they release it, it walks off of a fire escape and is killed.

"The Aztec Dog" was selected for the *Prize Stories of 1962: The O. Henry Awards* (1963), and is set in a Mexican hacienda where an aristocratic old gentleman, Fernando Iturriaga (the name seems to be of Basque origin), and a young, worthless American nineteen-year-old, John Anders, tolerate each other, mainly because of the old man's dignity and formality. The Aztec dog, named Vidal, belongs to Iturriaga but becomes attached to Anders, who feeds it bread soaked in aguardiente until it becomes drunk and then he taunts it. The dog is "of the ancient breed of alert Mexican mongrels from which the Aztecs had bred" other dogs and it has brought a gentleness into Iturriaga's life (115). Both characters have a flawed past, and events culminate in a series of adventures. The story ends on a note of sadness, for the lives of the people involved are tragic.

Graves moved from Mexico to the *llano estacado* for the setting of "The Last Running," which centers on a remnant of surviving Comanche Indians who want to run one last buffalo. This story of a last ritualistic buffalo hunt originally appeared in *Atlantic* in 1959, before Graves moved it into *Goodbye to a River*. Bill Wittliff, owner of Encino Press in Austin and publisher of collectors' editions of Texana, brought out *The Last Running* as a book in 1974. Graves says the story

> is based on an anecdote I once heard or read somewhere
> about Charles Goodnight in his old age, when a small band
> of Comanche Indians rode out from Oklahoma to his Quitaque
> Ranch below the Cap Rock to ask for one of the buffalo
> from a little herd he maintained so that they could run it
> and kill it in the ancient, traditional way with arrows and
> lances. (*Sonovagun* 6)

Graves justified the use of the tale when he spoke to members of the Texas Folklore Society in a keynote address in 1984. He said he was not a dedicated folklorist but a writer who uses folklore to make his own personal points (*Sonovagun* 3). For Graves, history retold becomes legend, because along the way in the oral recounting it loses its factual beginnings. He says writers are perverters of good folklore and history, and he believes "this is the sharpest point of divergence between genuine folklorists and people who are primarily writers" (*Sonovagun* 11).

One of Graves's earliest stories concerns an event from his military service. He looked back from 1954 to tell his story, "The Laughter from the Western Islands," about recuperating in a naval hospital

13

at Aiea on Oahu in 1944, after being wounded at Saipan. There is an ironic twist to the story as Graves comments on war and its waste.

Another story from this early period is "The Green Fly," about a young man who is at a quiet vacation spot in Mexico finishing a dissertation in English literature. He has a passion for fishing and meets an old doctor who joins him, and they develop a mild comradeship. As so often happens when civilization enters the peace of the garden, evil reigns. The story ends with an ungentlemanly act by a male guest but with the old doctor as the hero.

"The Off-Season" is also set in Mexico, in Acapulco before it became so popular with tourists, and it establishes a mood like that of a Hemingway story. The plot is about two men who had recently returned from the war and who "were still too close to the excitement of it to want to settle down" (26). Told in the first person by one of the men, the story has a happy tone until two women arrive. In a sense the men have run away from facing the future, and somehow the two women ruin their holiday by bringing them back to reality.

Graves returned to the American West for the setting of "The Dreamer." The action concerns a former mountain man, Joe McNeill, who has what Graves calls the "mountains' big lonesomeness" (28). At the age of sixteen, the redheaded youth, part Irish and French Canuck, drifts to St. Louis, becomes a trapper and hunter, gathers a pack of hounds and lives with them, and "if he was a little crazy, as the Utes thought respectfully among whom he settled for a while later, it was a craziness not uncommon in that age" (28). When his Ute wife is killed in a village raid by Pawnees, Joe leaves to seek white people, and the rest of the story concerns his periods of "dreams," for lack of a better term to describe his times of lonesomeness, when violent fantasies of death and destruction come to him. This rather long story, characterizing a man who never comes to terms with his inner world, reminds one of John Johnston, the Crow killer about whom Idaho novelist Vardis Fisher has written in *Mountain Man: A Novel of Male and Female in the Early American West* (1965). Like Fisher's, Graves's story departs from the traditional tale of Indian frontier raids on white settlers because of the portrayal of a protagonist who is not a stereotypic mountain man. There is excellent writing in this story, and Graves's dependence on history is subtle.

Graves has written a few other stories, but in the years when he was writing and publishing his books, he turned almost entirely to nonfiction. It is possible he will reach into the trunk, retrieve his unfinished novel, and complete it. He says he hopes he can, for he feels the greatest potential for a writer is in fiction; however, he has been most successful with nonfiction and the essay (Bennett 67).

In 1971 he collaborated in writing a Sierra Club book, *The Water Hustlers*, in which he criticizes water policies and usage in Texas. The editors of Sierra Club books state in a foreword that "moving water from where it was to where it had never been before" happened because water had to be where people were, and "That is how water hustling came to be the second oldest profession in the world" (7-8). Graves, writing "Part I Texas: 'You Ain't Seen Nothing Yet,'" says water hustlers do not take kindly to criticism. In addressing water plans for Texas from 1971 to 2012, he notes, "No single influence has more to do with the way Texas regions vary than the distribution of water" (19).

Critical of the ungentle use of the land, he would prefer the old Texas when vaqueros rode "out in the mornings long-stirruped and shielded in leather." He calls the Edwards Plateau "perhaps the Texas heartland," beautiful but less well-watered (20). The

15

discovery of petroleum and the influx of winter-weary northern immigrants he finds a blessing and a bane. Of real concern to him is the pumping by big modern engines "out of the Ogallala aquifer which underlies nearly the whole Texas High Plains," pumping for crop and pasture irrigation where once windmills took care of the cattlemen and dry-land farmers (21). He says that "more water is being pumped out of the aquifers each year than natural processes are putting back in as recharge" and that trouble is imminent where irrigation is heavy, as in the High Plains, sometimes known as the *llano estacado,* "a name of debated origin" (25).

Graves's geological history of Texas adds to our understanding of why he finds the water hustlers to be in bad form. He warns that the economy of West Texas, which depends on farming, may one day collapse when the aquifers are pumped dry. Further, he says it is a water problem not just in the High Plains, but wherever in Texas aquifers are exploited. Some of the industrial evils, such as river pollution, have been curtailed or stopped, but he does not find that enough is being done by conservationists to keep the land and rivers clean.

Graves concludes his study with a plan for wise use of underground water, but he has little hope for the Texas Water Plan as written, for "it is hard to believe that all the goals in something like the Texas Water Plan are sculptured with the guidance of sincerity and selflessness" (115). There is a need for better water planning in Texas, but Graves says, "more and more with time I find that the principal social and political thing I want is to be let the hell alone . . ." (115-16). He says he sees a lot of others like him.

Graves's concern over Texas water usage extends to one of his favorite streams, threatened to be changed forever by government reclamation projects. Thousands of readers have journeyed with him down the Brazos, a river haunted with the colorful, brutal history of Texas. *Goodbye to a River* is about a stretch of the Brazos River which winds across a number of counties west of Fort Worth, Texas. Graves's canoe trip actually traverses four counties—five, if you count Johnson County. The picturesque, hilly country is broken by creeks and valleys, in particular the Brazos and Paluxy River valleys. In its long course the Brazos flows into the Gulf of Mexico, traversing most of the main physiographic regions of Texas: the High Plains, the West Texas Lower Rolling Plains, West Cross Timbers, Grand Prairie, Blacklands, and the Gulf Coastal Plain.

The Brazos is the largest river between the Rio Grande and the Red River and third in size of all rivers flowing in Texas. The total length from its source to its mouth at the Gulf is 840 miles. The Spaniards called it *El Rio de los Brazos de Dios*, meaning The River of the Arms of God. Graves says, "local chroniclers have built legends around that name: that some strayed Iberians out on the drouthy plains shrank their swollen tongues in the river's salty pools; that a divinely-original head rise hissed down just in time to save a party's rear from whooping savages . . ." (17).

Most of the Brazos River lies within the boundaries of the Brazos River Authority, which controls a multipurpose program for the river's development. The largest reservoir on the Brazos is Lake Whitney; another is Lake Possum Kingdom; and the stretch of the river between these two lakes is the major concern of Graves in his river book.

The attractive format of *Goodbye to a River* was designed by Carl Hertzog, who was for years editor of the University of Texas Press at Austin. The book is organized into three parts with nineteen numbered chapters; some open with a pen and ink illustration by Russell Waterhouse, some with a quotation from a noted writer or philosopher. Included also is a three-page bibliography. The book is about people as much as it is about deer and ducks, squirrels

17

and sandbars, or plovers and eagles. Old tales mix with history and philosophic rumination.

The organizing factor is the river and the autobiographical account of a man with his dog on a canoe trip in the autumn in Texas. It differs from most books about river trips because Graves has more freedom to write about the folk as well as the history; yet *Goodbye to a River*, in its artistic creation, is not unlike some of the Rivers of America series books such as Stewart H. Holbrook's *The Columbia* (1962), Edgar Lee Masters' *The Sangamon* (1942), and Marian Templeton Place's *Buckskins and Buffalo: The Story of the Yellowstone River* (1964).

There is no indication that Graves was influenced by the Rivers of America series. In fact the ideas for his book came about when he was doing research on old log cabins in the Fort Worth area and he learned that the natural flow of the Brazos, the river he had known as a boy, was to be interrupted by a number of Brazos River Authority projects. To preserve his memory of the river he decided to make one more trip and on Armistice Day, 1957, he began a three-week canoe trip down a 175-mile stretch between Possum Kingdom almost to the headwaters of Lake Whitney. His sole companion was a dachshund pup that was named Watty but which he calls Passenger. He persuaded the editor of *Sports Illustrated* magazine to underwrite the trip; however, the finished essay was, he said, "not sporty enough for them," and although an advance had been paid, the magazine rejected it. *Holiday* magazine accepted it under the title, "Farewell to a River," but Graves recalls that "By the time it was over, there was a great deal more than just a magazine article there, and I just went ahead and wrote the book" (Holley 43).

Good books about Texas rivers are scarce, and *Goodbye to a River* joins Paul Horgan's *Great River: The Rio Grande in North*

American History as the two best books about Texas rivers. Horgan's book is a two-volume history that covers the entire length of the Rio Grande as man knows or has known about it. Graves's book covers but a short stretch of the Brazos; as he says:

> I don't mean the whole Brazos, but a piece of it that has had meaning for me during a good part of my life. . . . A hundred and fifty or 200 miles of the river toward its center on the fringe of West Texas, where it loops and coils snakishly from the Possum Kingdom dam down between the rough low mountains of the Palo Pinto country, into sandy peanut and post-oak land, and through the cedar-dark limestone hills above a new lake called Whitney. (4-5)

Graves dedicated *Goodbye to a River* to his eldest daughter, Helen, "who came along at about the same time. I hope the world she will know will still have a few rivers and other quiet things in it" (vi).

At first glance one realizes that the river book is not merely another story about Texas. Graves, writing in first person, informs the reader that most of what he is telling actually happened, but adds,

> Though this is not a book of fiction, it has some fictionalizing in it. Its facts are factual and the things it says happened did happen. But I have not scrupled to dramatize historical matter and thereby to shape its emphases as I see them, or occasionally to change living names and transpose existing places and garble contemporary incidents. (*Goodbye*, A Note)

Goodbye to a River is history, folklore, fiction, biography, and travel narrative. It is a synthesis of tale spinning, nature writing, and philosophical meditation. Graves says the essence of his return to Texas from his travels to Mexico, Europe, and New York is in *Goodbye to a River*, although he did not realize it at the time he was writing it, and he adds that in the writing of the book he found his tone of voice. But finding his voice took place only after a lot of apprentice work and fifteen years of searching.

After traveling about the world, he philosophically looks at one river, and unwilling to call change progress he observes:

To note that our present world is a strange one is tepid, and it is becoming a little untrue, for strangeness and change are so familiar to us now that they are getting to be normal. Most of us in one way or another count on them. . . . (8)

Still, he finds that "one river, seen right, may well be all rivers that flow to the sea" (254). It is this seeing that makes his account of the Brazos so original—that and the fact that he seems attached to this particular place and particular society, yet he can transcend it and make his place and society stand for all places and all of the societies in the world. His river becomes everyone's river. As he says, "One man's provincialism is another man's universality"; and like Thoreau, his musings also enlarge his writings.

Saint Henry, as Graves refers to Thoreau, "was a real ascetic" and enjoyed an austere life. Graves appears more pragmatic in his approach, and on the river trip he lives off of the land, regretting that he must shoot a duck, but satisfied that it was not a deer. He recalls that "Saint Henry David Thoreau, incisive moral anthropomorphist that he was, implied that blood sports were for juveniles, not men, and was conceivably right" (53-54). Commenting on the attitude of another author, he writes, "Prince Ernest Hemingway implies the opposite . . ." (54). Yet Graves dislikes destroying any of nature's gentle wildness. Like Thoreau, he has learned to listen to nature: the screech of the owls is not a screech at all, but a wail; and the whicker of the upland plover flying under low clouds on their way to Argentina from near the Arctic Circle has special meaning to him. In a meditating moment he says the whicker of a plover may not "touch all other men in their bowels as it touches me . . . . But it touches me. And I care about knowing what it is, and—if I can—why" (160).

Whatever Graves has in common with Thoreau, the Texan's prose brings the Brazos vividly to life. The stream that he paddles is not the upper Brazos that meanders through broad plains where it once watered the buffalo. It is not the lazy lower Brazos where stately plantation homes like those of the Old South once stood on the river bluffs and where the Texas capitol once stood, referred to as "Washington-on-the-Brazos," before it was moved to Austin. It is the upper-middle part of the river that winds among rugged, wooded hills and that still retains a good bit of its untamed wilderness characteristics. What Graves writes about is what he sees and what he recalls from history, and he weaves a tapestry of blood and war, of the cries from savage Indian massacres, and of old codgers who have made their livelihood from the river. A true naturalist, he sees the sandpipers and cranes; hears the deer running through the oaks, and the night-prowling raccoons by the campfire. He captures nature in its minute particularities and adds to it a subtle, moving philosophy that seems to make the book almost better than nature itself, but he does see grim evidence of people's degenerating effects on the country.

As he paddles and floats down the river, he sees few people with the exception of an occasional hunter or rancher. Most of the livestock is hidden by the "unvanquished brush" except for the curious Angora goats which peer at him. He ruminates about the Angoras:

Whatever their effect, I tend to think they symbolize a further degeneration of the country; there is about them a smell of the burnt Near East where their breed began; they seem a portent. This region raised antelope and buffalo with rich

fat on their ribs once, and later its longhorns were the stur-
diest that went up the trails. Now the cedar has spread its
sterile shade in the flats where grass no longer grows.
. . . Goats and other such Mediterranean fauna—burros, and
magpies, and tawny water-thrifty rodents that live among the
rocks—somehow symbolize for me those lands that will never
again be what they were. (57-58)

Graves's pondering may seem pessimistic, but he is probably closing
on truth, the kind Americans tend to dismiss too easily. Ashley
Cheshire reports that "Graves has two overriding fears about
mankind and the earth beneath him, and they both stem from
what he thinks could happen when man gets too far from the
land. One is an economic-ecology collapse. The other is a wasting
of the spirit" (20).

Graves does not believe mankind can continue consuming as in
the past without putting something back. The specter of an ad-
vanced society in collapse, of a people no longer trying to survive,
is disturbing to him. As for the human spirit, he says there is
less and less a continuing search for knowledge and truth. "We
are becoming genetically satisfied," he told Cheshire (2).

Graves finds a spiritual lack in the white race that the Comanches did not have: "The People were not exclusive in terms of
race," for they were "for two arrogant horseback centuries," proud
winners until the white race almost annihilated them (18-20). The
record is not an admirable one, and Graves's attention returns again
and again to those first riders of the Brazos.

After he has traveled a few days, he slows down and begins
to enjoy the solitude and to meditate on many subjects. He recalls
the stories he has heard about the places he is passing or where
he camps at night, and he weaves them unobtrusively into the
book. Some of the tales and the historical events bear mention

for their tragic endings and their humor, for the frailties of mankind are to be found in every bend of the river. Few people outside of west Texas have heard the stories Graves knows that are a part of the river's history. He tells of

the murdered, scalped, raped, tortured people, red and white, all the proud names that belonged with hills and valleys and bends and crossings or maybe just hovered over the whole— Bigfoot Wallace, Oliver Loving, Charles Goodnight, Cynthia Ann Parker and her Indian son Quanah, Peta Nocona, Satank, Satanta, Iron Shirt. . . . (7)

When he reaches Shut-in Crossing he recalls a story told to him about a man named Davis who "homesteaded there in 1857, a year or so before the Comanches . . . began the really bloody fighting" (25). Davis laid a floor of the house for his bride, bringing the boards from Waco by wagon, and "it was the first floor in the Palo Pinto country which was neither flat dirt nor puncheon. They say she was proud of it, and a few months later she died in childbirth and John Davis tore up the floorboards and made them into a coffin . . ." (26). Graves muses about what happened to Davis, but apparently no one knows.

Floating along Graves sees a bald eagle "fierce-eyed enough for anyone's Great Seal . . ." and recalls how western sheepmen shoot them from airplanes. He says, "We don't deserve eagles; they will go" (29). At Ioni Creek he recalls the fate of young and foolish Jesse Veale who was the last man killed by Comanches in Palo Pinto County one day in 1873. Veale and a friend, Joe Corbin, were setting fish lines and they came upon some Indian ponies staked out in the cedars and took them. The Comanches followed and began to shoot. An arrow hit Veale in the knee and his horse threw him. Corbin escaped and rode for help. On return the white men found Veale sitting dead but not scalped against a double-elm tree, his pistol gone and "Comanche blood on the ground around him" (36). The party did not pursue the Indians until the next day. Graves ruminates, "One saw them heroic in size and posture, and transmuted them into myth, and tried in reverie and play to live the myth; it is the process that in this day has shaped the whole Western legend into a raucous lie flooding out from bluely glowing television screens" (37).

One of the sad tales concerns a letter Graves finds on the floor of an old deserted house: "It was dated April 17, 1899, and was from someone named Elnora in Hood's Cove, Kentucky, to someone named Addie." The letter ends,

> . . . I do not know where Time *goes* and when he said the other Day that it was *Twenny Five Years* since You All went out to Texas and I begann to cry, Dear Sister, because I do not *believe* that we are Like to see Each Other any more. . . . (71)

Another violent tale concerns the Ezra Shermans who were living on the frontier in 1860 when the Comanches were a threat to the early white settlers. The ordeal of Martha Sherman is unbelievably cruel and is a story only for the strong. Similar incidents occurred at Welty Crossing, Brannon's Crossing, and numerous other sites along the river.

The stories are mostly tragic and Graves has much respect for those courageous people who first settled that wilderness. An admirer of Walter Prescott Webb, who grew up on the west Texas frontier, Graves knows the historian's accounts of Indian battles and of the frontier settlement from the first explorations of the Spanish into this region. He also has respect for those who love solitude. A hill-country recluse named Sam Sowell is hounded one night by four ne'er-do-wells until they set his house afire. Sowell escapes and after recuperating at the home of a neighbor, he disappears and they find that he has returned to the hills to start anew. Graves admires such a character, one of many loners who loom large in the book.

Graves too is one who cherishes his solitude, and his memories of his own youthful waywardness are self-revealing, a revelation that results from asceticism, both a denying and a reaffirming of the self. In this regard he does remind one of Thoreau, especially when Graves says that as for asceticism, it is the "root and sap of the idea of my being there, on the river." Although he finds that Saint Henry's "spare cry of 'Simplify, simplify!' rings more alien generation by generation" (68), he gradually sheds his city softness and comes to revel in a new luxury of frugality:

> You run a risk of thinking yourself an ascetic when you en-
> joy, with that intensity, the austere facts of fire and coffee
> and tobacco and the sound and feel of country places. You
> aren't, though. In a way you're more of a sensualist. . . .
> You've shucked off the gross delights, and those you have
> left are few, sharp, and strong. (154)

Returning again to the history of the river, he gently chides scholars for insisting on "primary sources" and documentation while admitting that "Most of the stories are recorded" (141). He throws brickbats at several persons, including Edna Ferber, who deserves them for misleading generations of readers about Texas with her novel, *Giant* (1952). His account of the "Dignified Mr. Couts, later the big man at Weatherford," who called the bluff of four bully boys, is a tale with a happy ending for "In '66 he drove 1,000 longhorns to California, rode back alone across the plains and down the Platte to the Missouri with $50,000 in gold in his saddlebags, caught a boat south, and opened a bank" (141).

Old Man Willett brings out Graves's humorous jibes on religion in that part of the country:

25

Calvinistic fundamentalism and its joined opposite, violent wallowing sin, settled that part of the world and have flourished there since like bacteria in the yolk of an egg. They streamed in with the gaunt unaristocratic Southerners who predominated in that settlement, and you may like them or not, but there they are. . . . There is nothing like having a few Mexican Catholics around to dull the spines of the Baptist prickly pear . . . . There you breathed in the Old Testament, like pollen, from the air, and it produced its own kind of hay fever. (178-79)

Old Man Willett is like many of the people Graves talks to who live along the river: they are uneducated but have at least one book, and they stand firmly by their kind of salvation. Graves feels an outsider at times, for he says "my fundamentalism wasn't fundamental" (179). His respect for the proud, independent old man is evident in their conversation, but one feels Graves is relieved to be back on the river.

We can follow his route and locate the places he describes on the well-drawn map of the region he provides in the book. Where he stops varies with the terrain and the weather. One afternoon, with El Greco clouds overhead, he studies the sky as it changes and remarks:

Two long skeins of big birds flapped across that grayness toward the south—sand-hill cranes, grating out their castle-gate croak—and I knew what the air's muggy edge meant. Geese confirmed it, the first I'd seen, four snows in a little disciplined V, winging solemnly and soundlessly south. (98)

Departing from his thoughts about wildlife such as geese, he often brings Passenger into his story. He and Passenger have a small tent for protection against the rain and cold, and his accounts of the little dog's antics are amusing, although not always. For example, Passenger's encounter with a stinging insect sends him crying into the tent, and the next morning he is sick. Graves believes the pup has been stung by a yellow jacket, since the dog has had this happen to him once before, so he tucks the little fellow into his blanket. When they again return to the river, "the pup had curled himself to soak up warmth against the venom in his blood; sleeping, he snored thickly and jerked from time to time, but looked better than he had . . ." (240). The pup is a valiant little creature. At one place above the river Graves says there "was a fine grove of big elms and pecans; squirrels there charked at me, and when I stopped and let the pup run ahead, ignorant of his function, one came edging flattened around a tree trunk . . . [and] arch-leaped to earth and ran to another pecan, and the pup, startled, danced after him screaming with tentative bravery" (73). Graves adds, "He was an affable little brute, impractical but comic and good to have with me, philosophical under scolding and the occasional sleepy kicks he got when he wriggled too much in the bottom of the sleeping bag at night." He saw how the dog had matured in a few days, developing more than in weeks in town, "giving up his abject station at my heels to run about the woods on our shore excursions, learning to evade the cold by staying in the tent or by hugging the fire, sitting like a figurehead on the food box in the bow as we slid down the river in the long bright afternoons" (82). The pup died later under the wheels of a pick-up truck.

Graves's prose can change from the elegiac, as in the passage about Passenger, to the lyrical, as in the lines: "A canyon wren was singing there; one always is. They love high rocks above water, and the wild falling song itself is like a cascade" (41). Another time he describes a storm coming, "From the southeast, rearing to meet the blue-dun cloud's charge, a white roll of exactly similar

shape moved up," and "they met with thunder and the last red
tints of sundown flame-edged their fight. . . ." (115). On another
occasion Graves finds his heart's joy—an epiphany:

> The Brazos belonged to me that afternoon, all of it. It really
> did. The autumn-blue sky . . . the yellow-white air, the cedars
> and oaks green and gold and red, the rocks the size of
> buildings, the sun on my back, the steady, comfortable stroke
> of the paddling, mohair goats kowf!-ing at me from shore
> when they caught my scent . . . and the whistling birds
> and the unseen animals . . . [and] the big suckers that leaped
> and splashed . . . People's sounds and a consciousness of
> them touched me from time to time . . . but it was fall,
> and they weren't on the river. It was mine. (52)

Floating on the river or camped along its banks, Graves continual-
ly returns to thoughts about people and animals and nature and
what mankind is doing to the environment. He mourns for the
earth, rivers, creatures, and what is happening to them, and finds
it "unlikely to start breeding people who have the organic kinship
to nature that the Comanches had, or even someone like Mr. Charlie
Goodnight" (158), yet the Goodnights and Shermans and their children
and grandchildren, he says, have pretty well exhausted nature and
her resources. He notes, "The rosy preindustrial time is past when
the humanism of a man like Thoreau (*was* it humanism?) could
still theorize in terms of natural harmony" (159). He wonders, "With
possible death by blast or radiation staring at us like a buzzard,
why should we sweat ourselves over where the Eskimo curlew
went?" (159-60). Further he observes, "The wonder is that a few
people do still sweat themselves, that the tracks of short varmints
on a beach still have an audience" (160). Sometimes he becomes
disgruntled with his own caring and goes fishing, but if there are
bitter thoughts about the future of the Brazos, the land, mankind,

and the creatures of the land and rivers, there are many passages in the book that are of exceeding joy and sweetness.

There is so much in this book. Graves admits, "So many tales, and every time you go to that country you hear a dozen more . . . . Too many to put down here . . ." (282). Paraphrasing Andrew Marvell, he wishes "there were only river enough and time" (289) to continue the trip, but it must end:

I'd made the trip and it had been a good one, and now they could flood the whole damned country if they liked, chasing off the animals and the birds and drowning out the cottonwoods and live oaks and sloshing away, like evil from the font, whatever was left there [of the river's human history]. (295)

In his record of the human history of the river, Graves reveals a love for all of the region. It is a pastoral landscape, a "hard pastoral" straddling the ninety-eighth meridian, that despite its abuse by former inhabitants, is a beautiful place to him (Bradford, "Keeping" 190). His is a mixed response to the certainty that this is his last trip down the river and upon ending the trip he laments that "We will be nearly finished . . . when we stop understanding the old pull toward green things and living things, toward dirt and rain and heat and what they spawn" (262), but he assumes responsibility only for himself and hopes that others will find this meaning in their lives.

The critical response to *Goodbye to a River* has been generally favorable, sometimes highly laudatory. His contemporaries, A. B. Guthrie, Jr., Larry McMurtry, and Paul Horgan have praised his writing style, and he told Bennett that he claims to care most about the feel of words, to find himself drawn to word writers over idea writers (76-77). Mallory Young, who says he likes words, prefers to read the work of Graves slowly, for a slow-going book "has to have texture and substance, something to mull over and suck on sweetly as you go" (3).

William T. Pilkington writes, "The book's tone is mellow but honest, and the writer carefully balances flashbacks to the past with acute and unromantic analyses of the present" (21). Edward Weeks calls Graves's book a "biography of a river," and says, "Good books about Texas are rare" (110). A book critic writing in the *New Yorker* compares the book to Thoreau's *A Week on the Concord and Merrimack Rivers*, in the authors' summoning up of the past history of their rivers (22 Oct. 1960: 192). Paul Horgan declares Graves "is clearly and proudly a disciple of Thoreau" (8), a viewpoint that Graves has often disputed. Co-director of the Center for Texas Studies at the University of North Texas, Denton, and a noted Texas writer himself, A. C. Greene includes *Goodbye to a River* in his list of *The Fifty Best Books on Texas* (1982). Wayne Gard says, "It is a warm, moving book with many rewards for the reader" (6).

Timothy Dow Adams finds Graves's writing style "highly polished and literate, reflecting the wide variety of influences alluded to in chapter headings," including Thorstein Veblen, George Herbert, Chaucer, Wordsworth, Shakespeare, Milton, Yeats, and many others (234). Despite his literary ancestors, Graves's style is his own, characterized by a sentence rhythm that flows as easily as the river on which he floats and as unceasingly as the labor he expends on his limestone land.

And finally, in assessing *Goodbye to a River* as a literary work, M. E. Bradford writes:

[It is] neither novel nor memoir . . . [but] a conscious creation structured to serve its own ends, taking considerable liberties with the biographical and historic experience out of which it is compounded. ("Arden" 949)

Since Graves's river trip, little construction has occurred on the Brazos, with the exception of Lake Granbury. He laments the impossibility of keeping a free-flowing river:

But if you are built like me, neither the certainty of change, nor the need for it, nor any wry philosophy will keep you from feeling a certain enraged awe when you hear that a river that you've known always, and that all men of that place have known always back into the red dawn of men, will shortly not exist. (8-9)

Such controversial thoughts often occur to Graves, but for the most part his tone is light and pleasant, especially when he is running his "piece of the river," for he says,

In the clear water I could see the tip of the paddle . . . . Sandpipers flushed, and a kingfisher and a great blue heron. Hidden in the brush, chickadees cursed one kind or another of bad luck . . . and a redhorse sucker shot four feet clear of the surface . . . . (14)

The lyrical tone of the work is one reason *Goodbye to a River* was runner-up for the National Book Award in 1960, and won the Carr P. Collins Award from the Texas Institute of Letters for the best book of nonfiction published in 1960. When *Hard Scrabble* came along in 1974, it too won the Carr P. Collins Award.

If the theme of *Goodbye to a River* is passage through a riverscape, *Hard Scrabble* is passage into the landscape. Dedicated to Sally, the Graves's younger daughter, the book was partially written in time made available through a grant from the Rockefeller Foundation. Hard Scrabble is the name of Graves's home, which he says "is something less than four hundred acres of rough limestone hill country" (3). He says the name is not "shiningly original." Ulysses S. Grant's wife, Julia Dent, had a place near St. Louis, Missouri, that was named Hard Scrabble in 1854, and "there have been others as well, from New England to California." Grant did not write so eloquently about his wife's farm as does Graves, who says the name reflects "the way I feel about the work I have put into it and the existence it has imposed on other owners and occupants over the years" (3).

In an introduction Graves explains his purpose in writing the book, not as an "account of a triumphant return to the land, a rustic success story, but mainly a rumination over what a certain restricted and unmagnificent patch of the earth's surface has meant to me, and occasionally over what it may mean in wider terms" (5). The opening chapter gives the reader the historical background of Somervell County, which Graves has known from childhood, especially "The pretty exhausted Paluxy hills," where some of his friends lived. He says, in observing Hard Scrabble, that "over a period of time, with some jealousy, I watched it pass into the hands of a new owner, and then into those of a third, though unused still and unchanged" (43). When he finally purchases the land, he ruminates, not unlike Thoreau: "I had Hard Scrabble, the first part of it. Or it had me" (5).

His ruminations often expand into enlightening observations on the international scene, politics, and war; yet his distinctive voice always returns, sometimes with apology for his digressions, to the task at hand: fence building, clearing brush, experimenting with various grasses, and the ever-demanding husbandry of his livestock. Behind the present he is ever conscious of the past, especially the historical impact Anglo-Americans, and what he calls "The Owner-ship Syndrome," have had upon the American West—in particular, upon his own acres of limestone, cedar groves, and creek-bottom pastures. He does not care to be "cast in the role of what his fellow Texan, Larry McMurtry calls 'the sage of Glen Rose,' " because of his work to improve his land rather than as a writer about it (Holley 43).

"The Hard Used Land" is Graves's label for the area he knows well, for it is land which has been "pretty thoroughly battered by human use a scant century and a half after Anglo-Americans began to move forcefully into well-watered eastern and coastal regions" (*Atlantic* 92). The land is at the far edge of what was once the old Cotton Kingdom until overcropping, overgrazing, drought, and dry winds stripped away most of the surface soil. Graves places most of the responsibility for the abuse of the land on mankind.

Of Hard Scrabble, Graves asks the reader to feel and understand his gradual commitment to what he calls "the place," and hence he brings in a sense of the past with wonderful tales of local people who, like the author, live deliberately bound to the land. The related chapters tell of soil, goats, weather, insects, intruders, daily events, and memorable happenings. He gives a history of early settlements in the area; of his first work on the land; of the topography, trees, animals, and hired labor; of moving in and building a house, barn, and fences; and of a struggle to make the earth productive. In between the regular chapters are inserted digressions on a variety of topics.

"An Irrelevance" and "Another Irrelevance" are two such digressions, and they deal with his past experiences with people. He had digressed with considerable success in *Goodbye to a River* in order to elaborate upon stories heard, general observations, and personal memories. One digression in *Hard Scrabble* has to do with the Scots-Irish freeholders who carried on illegal whiskey making. Another concerns an Alabama Italian who dies while talking to the author when both lie wounded in a Saipan field hospital. A third recalls the author's visit, as a young man, with a Spanish peasant living on the Balearic Islands. "His Chapter" may concern Graves's alter ego: it is a long story about a man called "O.F."

for Old Fart, who differs from his creator in that he spends the last years of his life in a small bungalow on the edge of town where the only soil he has to cultivate is his garden. "His Chapter," as the author told Patrick Bennett, is fiction that "sort of wrote itself" (79).

The reader never feels that Graves finds working on the place is a chore, because the author enjoys his life there, and if there are setbacks, he can retreat to the quiet beauty of the hills, trees, and the pretty Paluxy River and Valley. By making fruitful again his "part of the earth's surface," he meets a challenge he truly wants to face. He is interested not just in cows, but in different breeds and which breed will thrive best on marginal pastureland; of bees and goats, he remarks upon their value to the land and crops. He notes that Hard Scrabble is a segment of the rough lands of the Tonkawa, tribal descendants of a latter pre-Columbian hunting-and-gathering culture. The Tonk Nation experienced the worst exhaustion of its lands in the 1930s.

His remembrance lingers in the cedars as he recalls the Booker and Kyle homesteaders and their beginnings. He provides a map showing the shape of Hard Scrabble, which resembles a flat-topped knight's helmet with the visor off (47). The three hundred and eighty plus acres appear considerable until one has a view of the size of Somervell County, which shows as a tiny speck on the Texas map and is the third smallest of the 254 counties in Texas. White Bluff Creek runs through Hard Scrabble, receiving smaller runoffs from various streams, thus requiring watergaps, which Graves says sudden rainstorms wash out regardless of how "ingeniously one may erect them" (51). But he likes the creek and its bends where boulders "twist the stream's progress and make it talk" (52). The stream has a personality and Graves respects its temperamental nature, which ranges from a pleasant useful flow to a flashy flooding destroyer.

Graves knew Hard Scrabble's faults when he purchased it, but he was also aware that White Bluff's ten-thousand-acre basin held good grass cover and had less bare gullied ground and fewer cedars than nearby property; still the land is sparse and the stream more of a liability than an advantage. He knows that when flooding it may maroon his family, but most times it is a magnet for all sorts of wildlife and is thus more valuable to him.

In more than a decade of involvement with the worn-out land, he begins with the rooted population: cedars, oaks, and other trees (he likes best the live oak); the scrub growth and brush, some poisonous, some useful, but all of it having to come under some kind of control. The groves of big cedar give him the most problems, but he admits they make good posts—and this thought sends him into a digression about their value and rightness. Despite the work of bulldozing them from pasture lands, he finds virtue in their clean, aromatic quality and in their durability as fenceposts. He informs us that the Shin Oak, called shinnery, is beloved of rattlesnakes in summer, and he wonders why, concluding that the snakes must like it because of its shade. "Lore attaches to most of these trees and bushes," he says (79), indicating those with medicinal value. He knows that the needles of cedars, "when they break off in your hands, too deep sometimes for tweezers, hardly ever fester as splinters and thorns are likely to do" (76).

Grass, too, is important on Graves's land and he discusses the worth of various kinds, including the lowly johnsongrass, which is

> one of the most thoroughly successful importations of live matter from the Old World to the New, rivaling even English sparrows and white men in this respect. Arriving from Turkey around 1835 and named shortly thereafter for an Alabamian who sowed it and sang its praises as hay, it soon became

the chief and most pernicious weed in cottonfields throughout the kingdom. (84)

There are better grasses—such as the Turkestan bluestem known to Texans as K.R., for the King Ranch was where the first stands were grown in America—but Graves finds that "johnsongrass in the right places is a first-rate forage plant" (85).

Graves's observations of hoofed and clawed creatures range from buffalo and antelope to the Syndrome's "varmints" and insects, and he fully assumes the personification of Head Varmint, referring to himself as the Old Fart, or O.F. Expressing an admiration for the red fox, a more cunning creature than the gray, he dwells briefly upon "non-pinkcoated" fox-hunters.

He watches for birds, as in *Goodbye to a River* when he recognized the calls of several different wrens singing at the same time. In *Hard Scrabble* he looks for the upland plover which pattern the sky enroute from the Arctic Circle to the Pampas, and he anticipates the trumpeting of the migrant geese and cranes, which he claims have more of eternity in them than most creatures. Snakes, armadillos, and bugs also catch his attention, for he finds that all things have some meaning in the whole design of nature.

While he may spend considerable time musing upon nature, his practical sense demands that he pay attention to his daily farm labor. Mexican workers have helped him on the land and in many of his building projects. His years spent in Spain and Mexico gave him a kindred feeling toward those who are willing to work, and he harbors no enmity toward undocumented aliens, noting they will do labor Anglos avoid. (In an earlier essay in *Holiday* magazine, he expands on the Anglo-Mexican border relationship.) His accounts of building fences, a barn, his house, and various other buildings often digress into amusing stories about his hired help, his construction ability, and good building tools. Occasionally Madame [Mrs.

Jane Graves] enters the story with a willingness to help and with what he says are "unsimple ideas" about the future development of the house, which he admits "has never really quit growing" (176). The original structure of solid stone will outlast most homes of "The Ownership Syndrome," as he calls them.

In building and fencing and farming, Graves has good tools and knows how to use them, musing that sometimes ghosts visit as one works, and that "Madame insists that a female one of these used to pinch her on the rump, not hard, for a time after we moved down to stay" (186-87). Most of the improvements have been made with his own labor.

In the chapter "War with Mother N," he expands upon the details of field labor at Hard Scrabble: plowing, clearing, seeding, husbandry of his animals, and his O.F. determination to go organic. For all of his efforts, he finds that "Much of Hard Scrabble's field land is 'ungrateful,'" and he is constantly reminded of the past by turning up rusted barbed wire, old bottles and cans, and other debris left by former owners (201).

If former owners have given him problems, some of his present neighbors, as well as his goats and the mannerisms of both, provide him with entertainment. Goats and mules must be the more intelligent domesticated creatures. Cows too provide an income, but hogs and sheep he does not raise. In the chapter on goats he discusses his war on dogs that are permitted to run loose and that kill his livestock. In addition to his love of animals and birds, he has an expert's interest in bees and gardening, and he says that "Besides being an Old Fart he also may well be an Old Bastard and dislike the mass of his fellow men heartily" (230). His reference is not only to himself but to O.F.'s in general.

The final chapter is Graves's assessment of what living and writing about Hard Scrabble means. He expresses his satisfaction with a job well done. But he does not have much hope that humankind will be true stewards of the soil, nor is he optimistic about the human world and its outcome. Perhaps living near a nuclear power plant does give one a clearer view of humanity's transience on earth. Even if so, Graves does not dwell on these thoughts and has little to say about nuclear power or about the Comanche Peak plant at Glen Rose, assuming a rather stoic attitude, yet finding that "the technology on which we lean may end by erasing us all" (180).

In a more optimistic mood, he hopes his work on Hard Scrabble will be profitable in many ways, but he knows that without care the brush will return to the hills and fields and the streams will continue to wash out the ten or so watergaps. Care for the land he states simply: "leave land bare as seldom as you can manage, control runoff and the effects of wind; be gentle . . ." (233).

Graves continues to live at Hard Scrabble, but says he no longer works as hard in caring for the land and livestock. One feels his contentment in the rose-tipped dawns, the jubilant chorus of the birds, and the hazy distance of hills and fields. His piece of the Tonk Nation has rewarded him in ways money never could. Few people reach that state in their lives, as he says, "Because you do not really cease to be what your young years made you, nor do you really want to" (257). Thus, if he did not learn certain things one needs to know early "for fullness," he did learn them late, and in this book he has shared his experiences with all humankind.

Added to the earlier response to *Goodbye to a River*, the reception of *Hard Scrabble* signaled that Graves had arrived as a major Texas writer. There is no earlier study of all his work, but the reviewers have looked with high regard upon both of his first two books. Skip Hollandsworth, commenting on *Hard Scrabble*, says that "the power of the writing was so stunning that he became almost a mythical figure in, at least, the Southwest literary community." M. E. Bradford writes, in a rather mystical review, that

By books like this *Hard Scrabble* are we brought once more into fellowship with whatever ineluctably is. . . . No one writes better of the uncertain rewards of husbandry for a man who knows these rewards to be uncertain. ("Keeping" 195)

William T. Pilkington says *Hard Scrabble* is "well-written, informative, and descriptively precise, but is weakened by lack of an adequate structural device that might have allowed for a more coherent work of art" (21). Edward Hoagland finds that in writing *Hard Scrabble*, Graves has struck "a tone that suits the book," and that it is "particularly fun to hear from John Graves, down on White Cedar Creek in the Tonkawa Nation" (2). Joe Holley writes that "The distinctive Graves voice is very much a part of *Hard Scrabble*" (43), and Priscilla Davenport says that *Hard Scrabble* is "an artistic account of country life and rural doings that Graves employed as a metaphor for the 'thing bigger than Texas that we all belong to' " (6G). Critics have been sympathetic to the book, as they have to all of Graves's work. *Hard Scrabble* certainly conveys his love of a land few people have treated with care or respect.

That Graves's limestone acres had been used up by former owners is clearly evident in Bill Moyers' Public Broadcasting television interview with Graves at Hard Scrabble in 1979. The program opens with an overshot of the Brazos River as Graves walks with a friend. The film brings to life the limestone rock, gullied clay, and scrub cedars of Hard Scrabble, and it shows how Graves has struggled to make the land live again. Graves tells of his work on the land over a period of twenty years, and of the dignity one finds in improving a hard scrabble place. At one point in the program

Moyers comments upon the nuclear plant at nearby Glen Rose and says, "You seem to have a certain humility toward change and progress," to which Graves replies he "would prefer to exist in a world without these things," but since they are here he "believes in trying to understand" why they are here (5). While Graves reads from his works, the camera shows various scenes at Hard Scrabble. The program is a recapping of Graves's life and writing career prior to the publication of *From a Limestone Ledge*.

If *Hard Scrabble* is Graves's passage into the landscape, *From a Limestone Ledge* is his farewell to the old rural ways. Most of the nineteen essays in the volume are a celebration of "the casual but constant observation of detail, the *noticingness* of rural life," treatises on the pleasures and hardships of doing things for oneself, and a nostalgic meditation on country ways. Many of the essays first appeared in the *Texas Monthly* magazine under other titles; yet the collection is unified by subject and place as Graves continues to tell "about two decades spent in fighting and loving a quite sorry piece of land," his hard scrabble acres near Glen Rose (*Limestone xiv*). In his preface he says some of the essays "are footnotes to my book *Hard Scrabble: Observations on a Patch of Land*, in that they are expansions or variations on themes found there" (*xiii*). That is partially true, but Graves admits that his "piece of land doesn't seem to wear your interest out" (*xiv*), for which we can be grateful, otherwise we would not have the chance to meditate over so many ornery, puzzling, difficult, disturbing, enjoyable, and damned disgusting problems that occur and recur on a farm where "a long time before I ever saw it, in the days of too much cotton and too many cows," it was worn out by abuse (*xiii-iv*).

From a Limestone Ledge is divided into three sections. In the first, "Coping," the topics considered are domestic matters: meat, winemaking, eccentric builders, fences, and junk. "The Hard-Used Land" is Graves's own label for the country he knows so well, and as noted earlier, it is no wilderness, since it has been ill-used over the century and a half since Anglo-Americans began migrating to the area. Thus his "little postage stamp of soil" is a geographical palimpsest. Graves adds that for him a pastoral landscape like Hard Scrabble's is the best setting for human life.

He once thought there was a time when he could "take one last walk over its rough surface . . . then could sell it," and though he says he still believes it, the reader does not (*xiv*). Although his frustration in restoring some vitality to a wornout farm comes out in this last book, Hard Scrabble is John Graves, and it may be a "sorry piece of land," but it is also a piece of one man's soul. Only someone who has been a true steward of the land knows what Graves feels and loves about his limestone acres.

In the opening chapter, "Notes of an Uncertain Blue Collar Man," he recounts his struggles to rewire the barn, dig a hole for a septic tank, patch a leak in a stock trough, and plumb a kitchen. He gives H. D. Thoreau short shrift: whereas the writer of *Walden* "had only his basic needs to look after and could dine with friends in Concord when he felt like it, as according to recent report he rather often did," Graves spends his days hauling, pounding, scrubbing, lifting, digging, and chopping—labor necessary to the restoration of his place (9).

After a few months of such toil, he says that "whatever it is that you are, in my case a writer, . . . you find that you've ended up a part-time, unpaid, and often unthanked jack of all manual pursuits" (10). On a farm there is always something to be done; and when keeping good fences again faces him, he wonders if a fence is built more to maintain "peaceable relations with neighbors" than to manage livestock (13). Robert Frost, in "Mending Wall," expresses a similar philosophy about fences, and Graves admits that "what working and worrying with fences over a period of time does to you is to turn you into a fence fanatic" (23). In Texas good fences make good neighbors.

In the book's second section, "Creatures," he finds that cows and goats can be a problem, but they can also be a blessing. Although goats do not matter much to Texans, he says, "I seem to visit goats" (102) and he has a few good words to say in their favor, especially Angoras for their valuable hair. Their chief predators, aside from man, are coyotes and dogs, for they are fairly immune to disease and are good foragers.

Graves focuses on chickens as well as on goats, and his essay "Some Chickens I Have Known" gives some entertaining advice to the small-farm owner such as Graves considers himself to be, although he says he is "not a Chicken Fun and Profit type" (138). Raising chickens provides some amusement for him, unlike the sad hero in Sherwood Anderson's story, "The Egg." The coons, foxes, ringtails, and other wild creatures get most of his small flock, and in recalling one such scene regarding his chickens, he found that it

held a sort of Oriental tragic magnificence, with the monarch and three of his wives lying gorily decapitated on the throne-room floor while the rest of the harem ran around in circles and screamed about their loss, or maybe just about their fear. But mainly what its magnificence aroused in me was the rage of a bilked peasant; I was not far in spirit from those Chaucerian villagers who with clubs and trumpets ran and "skriked and howped" vainly behind Russell the fox as he dashed off with cock Chantecleer in his jaws, except that there was nothing to skrike at. (141-42)

Nevertheless, he sat up part of the next night at a window with a shotgun and when the foul regicide returned for more heads, blasted it away. Graves tried raising fighting cocks, but they too fell prey to the wild creatures of the night, despite the fact that they were bred to be ferocious by humans who may have extended their own ferocity, "which may well be the worst kind of all" (149). It was not difficult for Graves to give up the raising of poultry, although he found the game chickens truly beautiful in their ferocity.

Graves's essays on bees and chickens are small classics, but the finest story in *From a Limestone Ledge* is "Blue and Some Other Dogs," which has been beautifully reissued as a separate book by Encino Press of Austin. The story first appeared in the *Texas Monthly*, and references to the dog, Blue, may be found in *Hard Scrabble*. Blue, the best dog Graves says he has ever owned, disappears and Graves never finds him. He feels sorrow and the loss leaves an emptiness in his life. The story is a memorial to the dog, who never wandered from home. Graves knows that "In the country wandering dogs are an abomination . . . nearly always dying sooner or later from a rifle bullet or buckshot or poison bait, well enough deserved," but Blue was not such a dog (116). It is a beautifully designed story, based upon facts, although most critics have called it fiction.

From his lyrical story on Blue, Graves moves on to section three, "Ponderings, People and Other Oddments." In "Noticing," he returns to the uncertainties of existence and ruminates about a time when he lived in New York City and heard mostly the sounds of traffic. He questions which sound better: bawling cows or roaring traffic, and knows that cows get one's immediate attention. As he contrasts that time to the *noticingness* of his rural life, he admits to liking some cities, yet the country attitude differs: "It comes from having a personal stake in the landscape that envelops you, in the various beasts and fowls and crops and objects it contains whose ownership you claim, and in the activities of many wild things that own themselves" (155).

In the mornings, from the time one closes the house door until one returns at night, and often into the night, there is something on a farm that needs attention. One notices the bugs, a bawling cow, a washed-out watergap, a sick calf, an influx of black widow spiders, the sudden anger of bees too rich for their own welfare, and the weather. All of these concerns Graves attributes to the rural attitude of noticing, "Because if you grow careless about what's happening on the land, you stand a good chance of ending up broke and back in town" (155). The difference between city and country awareness has to do with belongings. What one owns one takes care of, whether it is land, animals, or fences.

Graves finds as much satisfaction in building a good fence as another person might in searching for treasure. In "Coronado's Stepchildren," he tells the story of a pear tree which grows alone in the brush. It is an ironic statement of the fantasy the people hold in his region that there is treasure about and Graves amusingly describes the many vain hunts for Spanish silver and other legendary riches. The attraction, he says, is clearly in the hunt itself.

In the final essay, "The Loser," he details an event all too familiar to many farmers: the foreclosure auction of the farm goods of a man who could not succeed on his one hundred and twenty-five acres. Graves calls the event "someone's ruptured love affair with the soil" (22). He realizes after attending the auction and departing early in a guilty frame of mind, that "The Loser had made us view the fragility of all we had been working toward, had opened our ears to the hollow low-pitched mirth of the land against mere human effort" (228). It is a sobering finale for Graves, whose emotional response to the land is revealed in his autobiographical account of years spent on a limestone hill country acreage.

Overall, the essays in *From a Limestone Ledge* concern how one countryman coped and survived. While ruminating, he has interests that go beyond the personal to what country life does for men in general, what Graves calls "the lasting statements of self" (Grant 11). As with his first two books on the Brazos, the critical response to *From a Limestone Ledge* was favorable. Maria Lenhart notes that "The raw material for these essays . . . comes from a keen ability to discern the wonder of even the lowliest aspects of his surroundings" (17). Evelyn G. Callaway finds that "his delightfully fresh figures of speech and literary allusions reveal his cosmopolitan and urbane background. He writes of homely country subjects with wit and keen observation" (2404).

From a Limestone Ledge is illustrated with drawings by Glenn Wolff that combine the rustic with humor, as do the illustrations by Russell Waterhouse for *Goodbye to a River*. Only John Groth's drawings for *The Last Running* seem too romantic for the prose style.

When Graves published *From a Limestone Ledge* in 1980, he had completed his "Trilogy on the Brazos." In the criticism that has appeared on his work, the focus has been on the individual books. With the addition of the third volume to his observations on country living in north central Texas, it will now be possible to consider them as a coherent whole, for the three give an intimate portrait of a landscape and culture as perceived and lived in by the author. As one critic points out, Graves takes the mundane details and shapes them into something not at all mundane (Lenhart 17). His view has been a study of the human history of the hill country of north central Texas, especially the land-use practices of its inhabitants from "The People" (Comanche Indians) through the frontier settlers to the farmers of his own time and to a type of landowner he describes as "a rural dilettante."

Graves's greatest achievement to date is clearly his Brazos books, yet ironically he has said he feels the highest potential for a writer lies in fiction. He prefers not to comment on the subject matter of the novels in his trunk, but one hopes that he will one day publish them. Even if he does, his Brazos books will undoubtedly continue to bring him recognition, for while living in Spain and Europe Graves realized that if he were "to do anything worthwhile as a writer it would have to be in terms of people and country" that he understood (Walts 10).

The country Graves understands is Texas, and his major work has been set within the borders of the state. He is clearly a regional writer. In response to the question of why the Southwest is important to a writer, Graves notes that when one looks "at a given region in terms of its literature," two important questions arise: "whether the region and its writers are distinctive enough to deserve to be looked at separately from the main body of literature and culture to which they belong . . . [and] whether the region's literature deserves to be called literature" (Walts 5). He feels restricting himself to Texas has been important for his work, because he believes his region is deserving of being written about and he says there is good literature about the Southwest. The region is distinctive and lends itself to strong interpretation not only because the landscape is so various and beautiful, but also because its people are so disparate, with Poles, Germans, Mexicans, Swedes, and others providing a kaleidoscope of cultural themes—not only for fiction, but also for poetry, music, dance, and other arts.

Like other artists, nature writers too see the world in a special way, for they are engaged in a search for a rhythm in which they can perceive the natural world, and Graves says "it's a never-ending fight to find it." Thomas J. Lyon, in "The Nature Essay in the West," says that "A persistent theme in the western nature essay has been the need for civilized man, when confronting the wild, to develop clearer ways of seeing and a clearer consciousness in general" (*LHAW* 250). Graves's aesthetic view of nature is combined with a sense of history so that in his meditations he speculates on nature's splendor while questioning whether or not certain natural things will endure the demands of civilization. Always finding something new in his environment, he concentrates on the known and gives it an inner and outer freshness by capturing the wonder he finds in a hard scrabble land that a century ago was a different place. His nostalgic return to the Brazos is a realistic acceptance of change in an inconstant world; and as a dweller rather than a traveler, Graves has a secure place as an interpreter of the western region.

Not one to forget his beginnings in the rural West, Graves often pays tribute to his mentors, with whom he says he has a "familiarity and old attachment" (Graham 16), and Lyon too places him in the tradition of Dobie and Bedichek. Texas writers continue in the tradition of rural themes, and as Lyon points out, "pockets of wild land and the few remaining undammed rivers become powerful in the literature" (*LHAW* 222). Certainly *Goodbye to a River* is an introspective return to a stream that is doomed to progress and, along with other Western nature writers, Graves laments the rapidly disappearing natural West. Yet in his understanding of progress in a technological world, or as Lyon calls it, "technosphere," Graves writes with hope as well as pessimism, chiding the government and those who abuse the land, while remaining aware of its wild beauty and interpreting it for all who care. Many nature writers have been in the vanguard of Western travel, but few have settled in one place or have recorded their experiences with such bracing candor and consciousness of one's self and place as has Graves. The accumulated effect of Graves's writing is that he has helped to shape the heart's reply to the beauty and wonder of the American West.

Selected Bibliography

PRIMARY SOURCES
BOOKS

Blue and Some Other Dogs. Austin: Encino P, 1981. "Ol' Blue." *Texas Monthly* 5.12 (Dec. 1977): 184, 186, 188, 190, 192, 196, 198, 200, 203.

"Blue and Some Other Dogs." *From a Limestone Ledge: Some Essays and Other Ruminations about Country Life in Texas.* New York: Knopf, 1980. 115-36.

The Creek and the City: Urban Pressures on a Natural Stream . . . Rock Creek Park and Metropolitan Washington. Washington DC: Dept. of Interior, 1967.

"Folklore and Me." *Sonovagun Stew: A Folklore Miscellany.* Ed. Francis Edward Abernethy. Dallas: Southern Methodist UP, 1985. 2-11.

From a Limestone Ledge: Some Essays and Other Ruminations about Country Life in Texas. New York: Knopf, 1980. Austin: Texas Monthly P, 1985.

Goodbye to a River, A Narrative. New York: Knopf, 1960. Condensed rpt. *Southwest Writers Anthology.* Austin: Steck-Vaughn, 1967. New York: Sierra Club/Ballantine, 1971. Lincoln: U of Nebraska P, 1977. Austin: Texas Monthly P, 1985.

Foreword. *Gringos in Mexico: One Hundred Years of Mexico in the American Short Story.* Ed. Edward Simmen. Fort Worth: Texas Christian UP, 1988.

Hard Scrabble: Observations on a Patch of Land. New York: Knopf, 1974. Austin: Texas Monthly P, 1985.

Home Place: A Background Sketch in Support of a Proposed Restoration of Pioneer Buildings in Fort Worth, Texas. Fort Worth: Pioneer Texas Heritage Committee, 1958.

Introduction. *Landscapes of Texas: Photographs from Texas Highways Magazine.* College Station: Texas A&M UP, 1980.

The Nation's River. Washington: GPO, 1968.

"The Old Guard: Dobie, Webb, and Bedichek." *The Texas Literary Tradition: Fiction, Folklore, History.* Ed. Don Graham, James W. Lee, and William T. Pilkington. Austin: College of Liberal Arts of the University of Texas and the Texas State Historical Association, 1983. 16-25.

"Recollections of Childhood." *Growing Up in Texas.* Austin: Encino P, 1972.

"Recollections of a Texas Bird Glimpser." *Of Birds and Texas.* With Scott Gentling and Stuart Gentling. Fort Worth: Gentling Editions, 1986.

"A River and a Piece of Country: A Potomac Essay." *Potomac Interim Report to the President.* Washington DC: Dept. of Interior, 1966. 51-61.

"The Southwest as the Cradle of the Writer." *The American Southwest: Cradle of Literary Art.* Ed. Robert W. Walts. San Marcos: Southwest Texas State UP, 1981. 5-20.

Text. *Texas Heartland: A Hill Country Year,* with photographs by Jim Bones, Jr. College Station: Texas A&M UP, 1975.

"The Thirty Year Fence." *Why Work.* Palo Alto: Behavioral Research Laboratories, 1966.

"Texas: You Ain't Seen Nothing Yet." *The Water Hustlers.* With Robert H. Boyle and T. H. Watkins. New York, San Francisco: Sierra Club, 1971. 15-129.

SHORT FICTION

"The Aztec Dog." *Colorado Quarterly* 9.1 (1960): 31-46. *Prize Stories of 1962. O. Henry Awards.* Garden City: Doubleday, 1963. 201-16. *A Part of Space: Ten Texas Writers.* Ed. Betsy Feagan Colquitt. Fort Worth: Texas Christian UP, 1969. 113-26.

"The Dreamer." *Readers & Writers* May-June 1966: 25-32.

"The Green Fly." *Town and Country* 108.4379 (1954): 79, 120, 124-27. *Prize Stories of 1955. O. Henry Awards.* Garden City: Doubleday, 1955. 215-25.

"In the Absence of Horses." *Escapade* 6.4 (1961).

"The Last Running." *Atlantic Monthly* 203.6 (1959): 39-45. *The Best American Short Stories 1960.* Boston: Houghton, 1960. Austin: Encino P, 1974.

"The Laughter from the Western Islands." *Colorado Quarterly* 2.3 (1954): 327-39.

"The Off Season." *Stateside* 11 Nov. 1947: 26-28.

"Quarry." *New Yorker* 8 Nov. 1947: 89-90.

ARTICLES

"Aunt Clara's Luminous World." *American Heritage* 21.5 (1970): 46-48.

"Big River." *Texas Monthly* June 1982: 116-18, 121-27, 212, 214.

"The Brazos of the Northwest Texas Frontier, Today." *West Texas Historical Association Yearbook* 34 (1958).

"The Bright New Waters." *Ford Times* Nov. 1964: 10-13.

"Carlsbad, the Incredible." *Holiday* Sept. 1951: 98-101.

"Dead Oaks." *Texas Monthly* Oct. 1984: 172, 174, 176-78.

"Drifting Down the Brazos." *Holiday* Nov. 1959: 32, 34-40.

"Drinking." *Texas Monthly* Mar. 1982: 128-32, 204-05.

"The Exhausted Land." *Texas Monthly* Jan. 1986: 50, 52, 54, 58, 60. *Texas, Our Texas.* Austin: Texas Monthly P, 1986.

"Going Under." *Texas Monthly* Mar. 1981: 134-37, 195-97, 199. "Fishing the Run." *The Ultimate Fishing Book.* Boston: Houghton, 1981.

"The Hard Used Land." *Atlantic* Mar. 1975: 91-97.

"The Heat Treatment." *Texas Monthly* Sept. 1980: 164, 166-68.

"Lord of the Flies." *Texas Monthly* Sept. 1981: 174, 176-78, 180, 182.

"The Lost Americans." *Holiday* Feb. 1954: 72-73, 75-78.

"The Overlap Land: Gringo and Mexican Meet in the Rio Grande Country." *Holiday* Mar. 1964: 74-75, 94, 96-98, 100.

"Rice University: The Pangs of Change." *Holiday* June 1964: 76-77, 162, 164-66, 170-72.

"Staying Alive." *Texas Monthly* Apr. 1978: 146-50, 152-55.

"U. S. Go Home." *Colorado Quarterly* 4.2 (1955): 117-32.

WORKS CITED AND MATERIAL ABOUT GRAVES

Adams, Timothy Dow. "John Graves." *Dictionary of Literary Biography Yearbook: 1983.* Ed. Mary Bruccoli and Jean W. Ross. Detroit, MI: Gale, 1984. 233-38.

Bennett, Patrick. "John Graves: A Hard Scrabble World." *Talking with Texas Writers: Twelve Interviews.* College Station: Texas A&M P, 1980. 63-88

Bogie, T. M. Review of *Goodbye to a River, A Narrative. Library Journal* 15 Sept. 1960: 3081.

—————. Review of *Hard Scrabble: Observations on a Patch of Land. Library Journal* 1 Apr. 1974: 1028.

Bradford, M. E. "Arden Up the Brazos: John Graves and the Uses of the Pastoral." *Southern Review* 57 (1972): 949-55.

—————. "In Keeping with the Way: John Graves' *Hard Scrabble.*" *Southwest Review* 60 (1975): 190-95.

—————. "John Graves." *Fifty Western Writers: A Bio-Bibliographical Sourcebook.* Ed. Fred Erisman, and Richard W. Etulain. Westport, CT: Greenwood P, 1982. 142-51.

Callaway, Evelyn G. Review of *From a Limestone Ledge: Some Essays and Other Ruminations about Country Life in Texas. Library Journal* 15 Nov. 1980: 2404.

Cheshire, Ashley. "John Graves: Life and Letters at Hard Scrabble." *Dallas Times Herald Sunday Magazine* 1 Aug. 1976: 1-3, 20-21.

Crume, Paul. "A Man and His River." *Dallas Morning News Sunday Magazine* 20 Feb. 1972: 22-25.

Davenport, Priscilla. "A Literary Trek from Hong Kong to the Kitchen Sink." *Dallas Morning News* "Focus" 3 May 1961: 6G, cols. 1-6.

Endress, Clifford. "Texas Literature: The Twists and Turns of an Enigmatic Tradition." *The Texas Humanist* 5.6 (1983): 3-5, 15.

Eyrich, Claire. "John Graves: 'Texas Thoreau' Celebrates Life Anew in Print." *Fort Worth Star-Telegram* 16 Nov. 1980: 1C, cols. 1-5; 18C, cols. 3-4.

Gard, Wayne. "A World of Its Own." *New York Times Book Review* 9 Oct. 1960: 6.

Grant, Lyman. "Books in Review." Review of *From a Limestone Ledge: Some Essays and Other Ruminations about Country Life in Texas. The Texas Humanist* 3.6 (1981): 11.

Greene, A. C. *The Fifty Best Books on Texas.* Dallas: Pressworks Publishers, 1982.

Hendrick, Kimmis. "Last Look at a Frontier." Review of *Goodbye to a River, A Narrative. Christian Science Monitor* 10 Nov. 1960: 11.

Hoagland, Edward. Review of *Hard Scrabble: Observations on a Patch of Land. New York Times Book Review* 19 May 1974: 2.

Hollandsworth, Skip. "John Graves: The Thoreau of Texas." *Dallas Morning News* 29 Apr. 1979: 6G, cols. 1-3.

Holley, Joe. "John Graves: A Master of Details and Ruminations." *The Texas Humanist: Ideas, History and Culture* 6.4 (1984): 40-44.

Horgan, Paul. "A Sort of Love Letter to the Brazos." *New York Herald Tribune Book Review* 9 Oct. 1960: 8.

——————. *Great River: The Rio Grande in North American History.* New York: Holt, 1954.

Kuykendall, Timmi. "Texas Writing: Work in Progress." Review of *Talking with Texas Writers: Twelve Interviews*, by Patrick Bennett. *Southwest Review* 66.2 (1981): 222-25.

Lenhart, Maria. "Making the Mundane not so Dull." Review of *From a Limestone Ledge: Some Essays and Other Ruminations about Country Life in Texas. Christian Science Monitor* 14 Jan. 1981: 17.

Lyon, Thomas J. "The Nature Essay in the West." *A Literary History of the American West.* Editor-in-chief, J. Golden Taylor; Senior Editor, Thomas J. Lyon. Fort Worth: Texas Christian UP, 1987. 221-56.

Pilkington, William T. *Imagining Texas: The Literature of the Lone Star State.* Boston: American P, 1981.

Ritchey, Mike. "Giants of Texas Letters Probe State's Literary Tradition." *Fort Worth Star-Telegram* 3 Apr. 1983: 7E, cols. 1-6.

Tinkle, Lon. Review of *Goodbye to a River, A Narrative*. *Chicago Sunday Tribune* 16 Oct. 1960: 3.

Weeks, Edward. "Biography of a River." Review of *Goodbye to a River, A Narrative*. *Atlantic Monthly* Apr. 1961: 110.

Young, Mallory. "On Reading John Graves, Slowly." *Texas Books in Review* 6 (1984): 3-5.

TELEVISION DOCUMENTARY

Moyers, Bill. "John Graves, the Head Varmint of Hard Scrabble." *Bill Moyers Journal*. Transcript PBS Special, 23 July 1979: 1-8.